Professor Birdsong's

77 Dumbest Criminal Stories

Leonard Birdsong
Winghurst Publications

Professor Birdsong's 77 Dumbest Criminal Stories

by Leonard Birdsong

Winghurst Publications
1969 S. Alafaya Trail / Suite 303
Orlando, FL 32828-8732
www.BirdsongsLaw.com
lbirdsong@barry.edu

Table of Contents

Introduction

Law Professor Leonard Birdsong lives in Orlando, Florida where he teaches Criminal Law, Evidence, and Immigration Law. He has written many scholarly legal pieces since joining the legal academy.

Among his scholarly pieces are his articles entitled: *The Formation of The Caribbean Court of Justice: The Sunset of British Colonial Rule in the English Speaking Caribbean* and *The Felony Murder Doctrine Revisited: A Proposal For Calibrating Punishment that Reaffirms the Sanctity Of Human Life of Co-Felons Who Are Victims.*

This is not one of those scholarly pieces!

This small volume of Professor Birdsong's *77 Dumbest Criminal Stories* is written just for fun and enjoyment. It showcases the kind of many funny and weird criminal law stories that he has found and written about since 2010. This book is a Free giveaway. Read it. Laugh at some of the stories and then go to Amazon.com and choose from his other inexpensive ten humor books for more such laughs. There are two series: *Professor Birdsong's Dumbest Criminal Stories* and *Professor Birdsong's Weird Criminal Law Stories.* As a matter of fact, you may find all of these other volumes at Amazon.com or by going to his website: LeonardBirdsong.com.

Enjoy them and have a few good laughs for my sake.

Professor Leonard Birdsong

Chapter One

Dumbest Criminals from Abroad

Professor Birdsong has had the opportunity and good fortune to have lived abroad for a few years. He is always amazed that Americans believe that America has cornered the market with respect to dumb criminals. We do have our share of dumb criminals; however, this first chapter will reveal to you that there are dumb criminals all over the world.

AUSTRALIA: *Peeping Tom?* A recent report reveals that a group of quick –moving nudists chased down a peeping tom on a beach and performed a citizen's arrest in the buff. Sun worshippers in their birthday suits spotted the perv allegedly filming them in Adelaide, police and the nudists said.

CHINA: *Something smells Fishy...* A company that spilled 10,000 pounds of catfish on a roadway in China still plans to sell the slippery suckers. The truck door had swung open, sending hundreds of fish flying into a street in Guizhou. However workers gathered up the seafood sprayed it off and packed it back into the truck.

ENGLAND: *They were the real Dummies.* Two British men who travelled to Syria to join the fight against the Assad regime were armed with copies of the books *Arabic for Dummies* and the *Koran for Dummies* face record jail sentences of 18 years after pleading guilty to terrorist offenses. Yusuf Sarwar and Mohammed Ahmed, both 22, may be released, on good behavior, for the last five years of their sentences under extended bail terms, ruled Judge Michael Topolski as he delivered the heaviest punishment to date in England for Syrian related offenses.

ENGLAND: *Could there be any evidence that the Queen had something to do with this?* It has been discovered that a species of hallucinogenic mushrooms have been growing wild on the grounds of Buckingham Palace, Queen Elizabeth's main residence. Filmmakers found the red and white fly agaric fungus as they shot a documentary on the 40-acre private estate. A British TV station has reported that "fly agaric is well known to contain psychoactive alkaloids.

ENGLAND: *He admits he was a bad buoy.* A former Royal Navy sailor admitted in court to stealing piles of water-resistant clothing because he has a fetish for the slippery material. "I get sexual gratification out of the feeling of the waterproof clothing on my skin," Alan Reynolds, 55 of Cornwall, told a judge. "I know it is irrational and I am sorry."

FRANCE*: Oh, what ecstasy!* Police arrested suspected drug traffickers after finding their stash of 26,740 ecstasy pills hidden in can labeled as pickles. The arrest was made in the town of Fresnes-Les-Montauban, near the Netherlands border. Police report that the seized pills had a street value of $253,100.

IRELAND: *The headline read: "Lettuce pray."* A thief in the night made off with 50,000 baby-lettuce plants belonging to a Dublin vegetable farmer who supplies local grocery stores. The unlucky Irishman said he needs to plant the lettuce soon or they will die and he will be at a major loss of another kind of green.

JAPAN: Tokyo police have arrested a man who admitted to landing a drone with low-level radioactive sand on the roof of Prime Minister Shinzo Abe's office to protest the government's nuclear energy policy. Police further report that the suspect Yasu Yamamoto, 40, turned himself in to authorities in late April of 2015. The drone contained traces of radiation and triggered fears of potential terror attacks. However, no one was injured in the matter.

LEBANON: *Red alert???* A security scanner detected radioactivity in a half-ton shipment of maxi-pads at Beirut Airport. The sanitary napkins, ordered from China, contained 35 times the "safe" level of radioactivity, government officials said. This is the latest in a string of radioactive goods coming into Lebanon.

NEW ZEALAND: *A not so funny fat joke...* A Pizza Hut employee got a little too saucy when she scribbled a fat joke on the inside of a delivery box. An irate customer was shocked to find the joke, which read: "How do you get a fat chick into bed? Piece of cake." The employee apologized, saying the gag was meant for a friend who had placed the same order.

NORWAY: *The headline to this one read: "Hair today, jail tomorrow."* Prosecutors contend that a man in the town of Hordaland was arrested for misdemeanor assault after shaving off his hair and beard and then attempting to glue it to the head of a bald man. The suspect contended that the recipient had consented to the act. The victim, who had a prior restraining order against the attacker, denied he had consented.

NORWAY: *He deserves to starve himself to death!!* The worst mass murderer in the country's history is threatening to go on a hunger strike until death unless he gets more prison amenities, including access to the latest version of Play Station video games. Anders Behring Breivik, who made the threat in a letter to the media, killed 77 people during a one-day rampage in 2011 that included bombing buildings and a mass shooting at a youth camp.

PERU: *We bet the Llamas were not unhappy about the taxi ride.* Llamas in Peru hitched a ride in a taxi to rest their legs – angering animal rights activists who called the travel method abusive. Giselle Aponte, 39 of Lima said she was transporting her furry workers because they were too tired to hoof it home after a long day of work. The activists say that stuffing Llamas into a taxi was a disgrace.

ZIMBABWE: *Former Rhodes Scholar and Harvard graduate hits the skids...*A convicted former Illinois congressman whose prison sentence for bank fraud was commuted by President Clinton in 2001 was arrested last year in Zimbabwe for allegedly making 100 pornographic videos and snapping 2,000 nude photos. Melvin Reynolds, 62, whose political career crashed in 1995 after he was convicted of statutory rape involving a 16-year-old campaign worker was in the African country while serving as a middleman for foreign investors. Possession of pornography is a crime in the country. In addition to pornography charges, Reynolds, a former Rhodes Scholar and a Harvard graduate, was also charged for remaining in the country illegally on an expired visa.

Chapter Two

Dumbest Criminals from NYC & the East Coast

Here in chapter two we now start our trip around the United States examining some really dumb criminal stories from New York City and other parts of the country. And, boy they are really dumb.

NEW YORK CITY: *Three true dummies and losers plead guilty.* Three Brooklyn men charged in a plot to join ISIS kill President Obama, and bomb Coney Island pleaded not guilty in Mid-March 2015 in Brooklyn federal court. Abror Habibov, 30, Akhror Saidakhmetov, 19, and Abdurasul Hasanovich, 24, all sullenly entered their guilty pleas. Saidakmetov was arrested at Kennedy Airport as he prepared to board a flight to turkey with plans to later to travel to Syria to join the terror group.

NEW YORK CITY: *Kiss of the spider woman, maybe??* A cabby who claimed he had a "no-kissing policy" in his yellow taxi was hit with $15,000 in fine for ordering two female passengers to stop kissing – and then shouting vulgar epithets at them when they got out. TV producer Christine S and her actress girlfriend Kassie T said they barely exchanged a peck in the back seat early into their ride when driver Mohammed Dhabi became enraged. "Keep that for the bedroom or get out of the cab," shouted Dhabi. At a recent hearing before an administrative law judge each of the women was awarded $5,000 for emotional distress, in addition to a $5,000 fine Dhabi was ordered to pay to the city.

NEW JERSEY: *A really creepy and desperate school bus aide.* A former school bus aide accused of taking lunch money and bagged lunches from preschoolers in the town of Millville has now also been charged with stealing cash from the bus driver. Rosa Rios, 33, was charged in March with additional theft and robbery counts. Police report that the new charges came after Rios had been earlier caught on a surveillance camera rummaging through students' backpacks. She was originally only accused of stealing money and food from the 3-to-5-year-olds she was supervising in January and February.

NEW HAMPSHIRE: *The headline read: "Transgender pol bombs out."* A woman believed to be to be the first transgender person elected to a state legislature was recently charged with calling in a bomb threat to a hospital. Stacie Laughton, 31, was charged with making the February threat to Southern New

Hampshire Medical Center that led to an evacuation. No bomb was found. Laughton had been elected to the state House of Representatives in 2012 but never assumed her seat after reports of a prior felony conviction raised questions of her legal ability to serve.

CONNECTICUT: *"Mary Jane was his real thang..."* A bag of marijuana fell out of a lawyer's pocket while he was defending a client in a courtroom. Vincent J. Fazzone, 46, was slapped with a citation for the stash, which contained two ounces of marijuana. A co-worker claimed the MJ belonged to the son of one of his clients.

WASHINGTON, D.C.: *The fox should not guard the chicken coop!* Fueled by an addiction to prescription painkillers, an FBI agent abused heroin from his own drug investigations and in the process ruined dozens of cases involving suspected drug traffickers according to details that recently emerged. Matthew Lowery, formerly a special agent with the Washington field office, will plead guilty to 64 charges of obstruction of justice, heroin possession and conversion of property.

MARYLAND: *The question was "SWATS" for dinner?* A supermarket shoplifter who was caught stealing hair accessories and a bag of chips thought she would escape store security by scaling the shelves and climbing into the ceiling of a Giant Food store in Baltimore. After ceiling tiles began to fall, the grocery store was forced to evacuate and call a SWAT team to extract the woman – who had taken merchandise worth $8.50. Nevertheless, they arrested her and sent her to jail.

NEW YORK CITY: *What a sting for a crossing guard, and it wasn't even real coke!* An on-duty crossing guard in Queens was arrested after being given a bag with cash and cocaine inside and failing to turn it in to law enforcement authorities. Bernard Pelzer, 58, was directing school children across the street when he was targeted in an NYPD integrity test designed to nab department employees for misconduct. He took a bag containing cash and white powder that looked like cocaine and tried to keep it. He was charged with petit larceny, official misconduct, possession of stolen property and possession of a controlled substance. *Silly Pelzer, he should have smelled a set up.*

NEW YORK CITY: *What kind of idiot wears a teddy-bear hat to an armed robbery?* A man dressed in a teddy-bear hat and armed with a large knife tried to rob a woman in the lobby of her Manhattan building. The 31-year-old victim had just exited a subway station when the suspect started trailing her. When she entered the lobby of her building he followed her inside, pulled a butcher knife and demanded her purse and valuables. She fought him off and he fled. NYPD put out a look out for the suspect described as being about 25 years old, 5-foot-5 and 130 pounds, who was last seen wearing beige knitted teddy-bear hat and a camouflage jacket.

NEW YORK CITY: *Do not send in the clowns...* It has been reported that two clowns were led out of the Times Square subway station in handcuffs under arrest in early February of this year for annoying subway riders. Andrew Valins, 37, and Gordon Reintis, 42, were trying to get some laughs from stone-faced subway riders while dressed as clowns on the Times Square-Grand Central shuttle. The men wearing white face paint and big red noses were walking up and down the train car while trying to get riders to eat from a bowl of peanuts. A few passengers got off the train and reported the clowns to patrol officers. Valins and Reintis were charged with loitering.

NEW YORK CITY: *Sounds like grandpa needs his eyes checked.* A 79-year-old man who thought he was picking up his great-grandchild from school picked up the wrong child and did not realize the mix-up until his wife saw the kid. When the grandpa pulled into his garage the child refused to get out of the car. The man went into the house and got his wife who took off the child's hat and realized that the great-grand father had picked up the wrong child. The wife immediately called the school. It is reported that the two kindergarten boys were wearing similar hats, the same color coats and are about the same size. It was further reported that police are investigating the matter.

NEW YORK CITY: *Angel, you are a dangerous blockhead!* Angel Flores, 47, went ballistic because he did not like the photos of him that his girlfriend had posted to her Facebook. He demanded that she take the photos down. When she did not do so right away, he grabbed her 2-year-old daughter and threatened to throw her from the 10th-floor balcony of the girlfriend's Staten Island apartment. He then pulled a knife on the girlfriend and next ripped a television off a wall and stomped it to bits. Police were called. The woman and child were not seriously injured and Flores was arrested for criminal mischief, weapon possession and endangering the life of a child.

NEW YORK: *A very, very strange kitty case, indeed!* A man was arrested in late 2014, in connection with the April discovery in Yonkers of 25 dead cats hanging from trees in plastic bags, a grisly find that led cat lovers to post $25,000 in reward money. Westchester

County's Society for the prevention of Cruelty to Animals, which offered the reward, said Rene Carcamo, 60, of Yonkers was charged with illegally disposing of the cats but not with killing them. Carcamo was also charged with animal cruelty after a vet found that two kittens in his possession were severely neglected.

NEW YORK: *Oh deer, oh deer! Someone needs glasses!* A man who shot a deer in the Hudson Valley woods was hauling it away in a cart when he was wounded by a second hunter firing at the dead animal. The second hunter who thought the moving deer was alive, struck the first hunter in the hand and the buttocks, according to a report from the duchess County police. The injured hunter was treated and released from the hospital. No word on whether charges are being brought against the second hunter.

CONNECTICUT: *Police labeled it as plain old naked rage...* A stripper angry at being stiffed on tips allegedly trashed the Ruby II bar in Bridgeport and assaulted patrons. Fran Ruiz, 28, also threw bottles around and kicked the bouncer in the groin. Witnesses reported that as she was being handcuffed, she spit in the officer's faces. A real hellcat!

PENNSYLVANIA: *What an imbecile!* A man tried passing counterfeit $20 bills at the wrong yard sale, according to a report by police authorities. Grey Douglas, 40, has been charged with forgery, uttering and theft by deception after he tried to hand the fake money to the woman running the sale – who just happened to be a bank teller. Amy Miller who works at a Citizens Bank said that the phony bills were not printed on real "money paper" that she handles every day at work.

MASSACHUSSETTS: *That old rugged cross!* A mixed-martial-arts fighter was arrested for allegedly beating two men he strapped to a cross. Vito Resto of Springfield hung his victims on the makeshift cross and pummeled them for a "misdeed in the drug trade," reports say. Resto, a top fighter who has a tattoo of Christ on one shoulder, pleaded not guilty to kidnapping, assault and battery charges.

MASSACHUSSETTS: *What a crazy way to waste bacon and sausages!* Lindsey McNamara made headlines in Framingham last December 26, when she was caught on video hurling bacon and sausages in a police station, saying "It's time to feed the piggies." She was charged with malicious destruction of property. However, a judge dismissed the charge, ruling police had failed to show any damage. Still, she did have to pay $150 for her disorderly conduct.

NEW HAMPSHIRE: *They say this guy made a "grave mistake."* Michael Day, 38, pleaded guilty to helping a female friend to dig up her father's grave in hopes of finding his "real will." No will was found, but a bottle of vodka, cigarettes and cash were swiped by the grave robbers.

Chapter Three

Dumbest Criminals from Florida & the South

Professor Birdsong lives in Orlando, Florida. He loves the weather and the people here but Florida has more than its share of dumb criminals. Enjoy some of their stories.

FLORIDA: *As thin as an Auschwitz prisoner!* A woman was charged with neglect after the 96-year-old man she was supposed to be caring for showed up at a hospital so malnourished that he was just "skin and bones" and weighed only 89 pounds according to Apopka police. The man told police that his caretaker Alice K, 56, threatened to feed him dog feces and refused to let him eat. Police report that the doctor at the Florida Hospital Apopka likened him to an "Auschwitz prisoner." Police further reported that the man had been fed very little, if at all, over the last month. Upon being admitted the hospital called the Department of Children and Families which then contacted the police. When he was fed at the hospital he starting eating like a "starving dog," according to the treating doctor. Alice K was charged with neglect of an elderly person and was taken to the Orange County Jail and held on $500 bond. The elderly man remains in the hospital and will eventually be released to the care of DCF police said.

FLORIDA: *Unfortunately, sounds like gay sex-slave prostitution is alive and well in*

Florida! A Hungarian man has been convicted in South Florida for his role in running what investigators called a gay sex-slave prostitution ring. Andras Janos Vass faces a minimum of 21 years and a maximum of 155 years in prison after a Miami jury convicted him in April 2015 of human trafficking and racketeering. Reported testimony from the trial revealed that Vass and others brought three victims to New York in 2012 and forced them to perform sex acts at all hours. The victims and their families in Hungary were threatened and the victims' travel documents were confiscated. The ring relocated to the Miami area later in 2012. We learn further that two other Hungarians are awaiting trial in the matter.

FLORIDA: *The headline read: "Their mouths were clean but their hands were dirty."* Orange County deputies allege that 64-year-old Mary Curtiss and 44-year-old Clint Curtis led a racketeering operation that was responsible for stealing more than $100,000 in electronic toothbrush products and cash from Publix, Walmart, Walgreens and CVS stories throughout central Florida. The criminal complaint further alleges that the bulk of the money the two brought in came from stealing two particularly unusual items—high-end electronic and replacement toothbrush heads – then returning them as if they had legitimately purchased and pocketing the cash. Not only were the corporations losing money in the stolen merchandise, but they also lost money each time their employees processed a return. The Curtiss's are being held in the Orange County Jail awaiting trial.

FLORIDA: *Like father like son.* A father plowed through a fence while getting driving lessons from his 15-year-old son – who also didn't have a driver's license, police report. Luckner Louis allegedly broke through a park fence in Boynton Beach and then fled with the teen. Both were caught and each was charged with criminal mischief.

FLORIDA: *Hacking, hacking, hacking...too smart for his own good.* A Pasco County middle school student was arrested after authorities said he accessed a school district computer containing FCAT information. The sheriff's office reported that the 14-year-old logged into several network computers using an administrative-level account for which he did not have access. Aside from accessing the computer containing 2014 test information, officials maintain the student took control of a teacher's computer and displayed an image of two men kissing, disrupting classroom activities. The teen faces felony charges of unauthorized access of computer systems.

SOUTH CAROLINA: *God and space aliens, oh come on!* A man and woman broke into Carowinds theme park in Fort Mill after closing. Fran Gee and Jay Lay claimed that God and space aliens urged them to break in, police said. They were charged with trespassing and child neglect when police found an 8-year-old boy alone in their truck.

FLORIDA: *Junkie High jinks??* It appears that heroin was the draw for dozens of folks who lined up on three flights of stairs at a condo complex in Orange County. Undercover agents had just discovered the heroin hot spot when a marked police car, responding to a separate incident, panicked the druggies, prompting some of them to jump out of windows to dodge arrest. No information on how many were injured or arrested.

KENTUCKY: *Deborah, you are a lunkhead. Certain things you just don't advertise in public!* Police in Kentucky found plenty of "probable cause" to arrest 37-year-old Deborah Asher who they spotted wearing a tee shirt that read: "I love crystal meth." The Laurel County sheriff's department arrested her on charges of trafficking meth. We learn that her mug shot shows her still wearing the tee shirt.

FLORIDA: *The headline read: "He only bought a one way ticket."* A Boynton Beach man who left his car running while he bought lottery tickets really does need the prize money now. Why? Because a thief stole his car. The unlucky 42-year-old was playing a scratch-off game when the bandit hopped in his 2004 Infiniti and sped off from the gas station and minimart.

FLORIDA: A robber broke into a kitchen at a beauty parlor and drank seven beers and a glass of cognac, according to a police report from St. John's County. The intruder or intruders worked up an appetite at Nails by Kim, because they then used the salon's outdoor grill for a barbeque.

LOUISIANA: *Yep, it all came out in the wash...* An accused murderer who broke out of a prison van's back window was captured after a three-day manhunt because he stopped to do his laundry. Lorenzo Conner, 24 of New Orleans, was being taken to a mental health facility when he slipped out of his shackles and fled. A tipster alerted police after spotting him at a suburban laundromat.

FLORIDA: *So how long have you had that headache, mister?* A bandit in Orlando broke into a convenience store by literally bashing in the front door with his head. The hardheaded crook shattered the glass at the sunshine Food Mart in Orlando and made off with $10,000 worth of scratch-off lottery tickets. The owner of the mart immediately contacted the Florida

Lottery Commission and all the scratch-off tickets were cancelled before any could be used.

FLORIDA: *We wonder what the young men were learning in this college?* FastTrain, a network of seven now defunct, for-profit colleges, used strippers to recruit students and coached students on how to lie on financial forms to obtain taxpayer dollars, all according to a lawsuit recently filed in Florida. It is alleged in the legal filing that FastTrain "purposely hired attractive women and sometimes exotic dancers and encouraged them to dress provocatively" to recruit young men.

FLORIDA: *The headline read simply: "Rats."* Animal rescue workers found that a Tampa woman's house was overtaken by more than 300 pet rats. Flora Brown, 36, had originally bought five pet rats that quickly began to multiply. The rats then began nesting in her walls and her furniture. It is reported that the animal rescue workers removed hundreds of the rats and are planning to put some of them up for adoption. *Rats!*

FLORIDA: *Temper, temper...* Police handcuffed a man who allegedly threatened to blow up a strip club after the manager tried to confiscate his beer. Ronald Bright, 50 tried to enter the Lido Cabaret in Cape Canaveral in December 2014, with an open can of beer when the manager stopped him. Bright also reportedly warned that he would shoot and kill sheriff's deputies if they tried to arrest him – but he didn't.

FLORIDA: *What a nincompoop!* A man held up a convenience store in Cape Canaveral – and left his wallet containing his ID. So Brevard County Sheriff's deputies went to the home of Benjamin Shaw, 25, and arrested him in connection with the $40 robbery.

FLORIDA: *We have reason to believe alcohol may have been involved in this one.* A young punk irritated workers at a pharmacy when he stripped naked and curled up in doggie bed. The 22-year-old man dragged the doggie bed into the bathroom of the CVS near Tampa and fell asleep on top of it. Police later charged the man with theft because the doggie bed was unsellable after the nude nap.

FLORIDA: *Only in Florida, only in Florida...* A Volusia County man accused of catching young alligators for a Super Bowl dinner beat the small reptiles to death with a hammer and used a power saw to hack off their tails. These details were contained in a report made by the Florida Fish and Wildlife Conservation Commission, whose officers charged Richard Nixie, 30, of DeBarry with taking and possessing alligators without a permit tag. The Commission also cited Robert Lewis, 26, Nixie's neighbor; allegedly he helped skin the gators and prepared the meat for cooking.

ALABAMA: *He told the tooth, the whole tooth and nothing but the tooth!* A truck driver claims he crashed his truck because he was trying to pull out a loose tooth while driving. He was ticketed by police. However, the self-employed driver presented the tooth to prove to police that the tooth was to blame. No one was injured. No word on whether the ticket was quashed.

FLORIDA: *Have it your way at McDonald's?* We learn that a frisky but inebriated couple was hauled to jail for having sex on the trunk of a car in a McDonald's parking lot. Police report that Andrea Pauling, 23, and Michael Marin, 22, were kicked out of a Vero Beach McDonald's after swigging liquor from a bottle, then for "getting it on" once they got it on outside.

FLORIDA: *When caught always blame the wife first!* It has been reported that a squatter lived like a king for two nights at a luxury Palm Beach resort – because nobody noticed him stroll into the hotel room. Norman Karwacki, 29, of Boynton Beach, relaxed in the laps of luxury for two nights at the $731-per-night Eau Palm Beach Resort and Spa, before making off with a wall mounted TV. He was soon arrested and told police he had been staying there because he had gotten into a fight with his wife.

FLORIDA: *Sounds like this kid may grow up to be a real pervert.* A teenager was arrested for posing as a pervy physician. The young doctor wannabe wore a white lab coat labeled "anesthesiology" at an OB-GYN office in West Palm Beach, a patient told police. The kid was arrested after his mother ratted him out.

FLORIDA: An elderly bingo fan became so angry when a police officer tried to remove her from a bingo hall in Delray Beach; she ripped his walkie-talkie speaker off his uniform. Julia Garabo, 64, had gotten into a fight with another patron, and was arrested when she put her hands on the police officer.

GEORGIA: *The headline for this one read: "What a panty waste."* A woman stole 785 pairs of sexy underwear at a Victoria's Secret Valentine's Day 2015, sale at an Atlanta mall. The bandit stuffed $10,000 worth of garments into three shopping bags and bolted from the store. She was seen on video wearing a red hat and red tennis shoes – appropriate for Valentine's Day.

ARKANSAS: *GIRDLE UP!* State officials took over administrative operations at the Little Rock School District February 1, 2015, after the state enforced an unpopular dress code for staff, which mandated that teachers wear underwear and bras to school every day and banned Spandex.

NORTH CAROLINA: *Would this have been a "cereal" killing if he had died?* A woman mistakenly shot her Fort Bragg soldier husband, believing he was an intruder after he returned home with a surprise breakfast for her. Zia S accidently set off the house alarm when he entered, waking his wife Tiffany, who then grabbed a shotgun and fired through the bedroom door. He was not seriously hurt. No charges were brought against Tiffany.

LOUISIANA: *Big stink???* It has been reported that Police in New Orleans are trying to sniff out a bad guy. He is a thief that stole 30 air fresheners from a Family Dollar Store, worth more than $200. It is obvious that the police would make a big stink over this case because there is a reward of $2,500 for information leading to the thief's arrest.

KENTUCKY: *Sounds like this might have been some kind of inside job.* Authorities stumbled on some backyard bourbon; however, this was fine liquor and not homemade moonshine. Franklin County sheriff's deputies found five barrels of bourbon stolen from the Wild Turkey Distillery. The suspect hid the stolen spirits worth between $3,700 and $6,000 per barrel, in his backyard, the deputies said.

KENTUCKY: *Yes, police threw the book at him!* A candidate for Kentucky lieutenant governor was arrested for failing to turn in a library book more than a decade ago. Johnathan Masters, 33, was driving to a TV interview when police pulled him over for having expired tags. The officer ran his name and found he had a warrant out for "theft by failure to make required disposition of property" eleven years ago.

Chapter Four

Dumbest Criminals from the Midwest

Professor Birdsong did not find many dumb criminals from the Midwest but the one's he has included here are dumb enough to make you laugh.

INDIANA: *A possibly explosive washroom!* In March 2015, a restroom at a Walmart in Muncie was closed indefinitely after an employee discovered a working meth lab inside. The Walmart employee alerted police after seeing a suspicious man enter the restroom with a backpack and leave without it. Police say that people are leaving "the deadly explosive chemical in public places," rather than risk explosions at home.

OHIO: *Hoist by his own petard.* A man in Alliance called 911 to report that his wife stole his cocaine and was then arrested himself. Officers responding to the call discovered the man had a marijuana pipe and that he was wanted on a warrant for failing to pay hundreds of dollars in costs in an earlier court case. The man, 39-year-old Robert C was charged with improper use of the 911 system and possession of drug paraphernalia.

WISCONSIN: *We smell a drinking problem!* A drunken driver claimed the reason police smelled alcohol on his breath was because he had just finished eating "beer-battered fish." Police found that John P, 75, had been driving around with an open can of red dog beer in his truck. Police report that Mr. P had nine previous DUI convictions and failed yet another sobriety test when they tested him.

IOWA: *OMG! "Poopsenders.com"* A woman experiencing bad blood between her and her neighbors is facing a stint in jail after mailing them a box of cow dung. We learn that Kim Cape, 41, used "poopsenders.com" to anonymously mail the dung to the neighboring couple after they repeatedly complained to police about her dog's barking. "After all the problems we've had, I thought it would be a funny thing to do," Cape explained to authorities.

OHIO: *He will probably keep robbing this bank until he gets it right.* A man allegedly robbed a bank that he previously robbed back in 1999. Larry Hewitt, 47, did more than five years behind bars for the robbery at the Ohio Savings Bank branch in Richmond Heights. Now he has been indicted for hitting the same bank in

November 2014, stealing $6,240, according to an official report.

MINNESOTA: *The headline to this one could have read" "This crime was a jug of bull."* A bandit stole $70,000 worth of bull semen from a farm in LeRoy. It appears that a storage unit in the farm's milking parlor was left unlocked, allowing the still at large thief to swipe the valuable material. Perhaps it was an inside job.

Chapter Five

Dumbest Criminals from Way Out West

Professor Birdsong has travelled out west many times. However, he never wanted to live out west because he doesn't like mountains or the lack of water out west. However, as you will see there are no lack of dumb criminals way out west. Enjoy.

OREGON: The headline read: "It was a grizzly discovery." TSA agents cited a man for unlawful possession of wild game parts after they found a collection of bear paws in his luggage. Hong-Shiou Chiou was arrested at the Eugene airport while trying to smuggle the illicit items to Taiwan in plastic grocery bags. Chiou maintained that the bear paws were for a necklace.

TEXAS: *At least he did not have "Gin & Juice" with Snoop.* A state trooper has been reprimanded for posing for a photo with Snoop Dogg at the South by southwest festival in Austin because the rapper has several convictions for drug possession. Billy Spears was working security at the March 2015 event when Snoop Dogg asked to take a picture with him. The artist posted the image on Instagram with the comment, "Me n my deputy dogg." Department of Public Safety and Transportation officials saw the posting and cited Spears for deficiencies that require counselling for a supervisor. Spears's attorney says his client did not know about the rapper's criminal record.

However, Spears can't appeal the citation because it isn't a formal disciplinary action.

WYOMING: *WHY?? Did they plan to open their own store?* Police report that a man and a woman recently stole more than $9,000 worth of women's undergarments from a department store. The shoplifters made off with over 1,000 Pairs of panties from a JC Penney store in Cheyenne.

TEXAS: *Dummy!* A San Antonio man visited his son in jail and ended up behind bars himself. Jose Gonzalez, 53, thought it would be no problem to bring his combination walking cane and sword with him to the county jail. The cane passed through a metal detector, which went off, and guards unscrewed the top of it and found the two foot sword inside.

UTAH: *They take protection of their wildlife very seriously in these parts.* Utah TV personality Dell "Super Dell" Schanze, 45, pleaded guilty to a misdemeanor charge of harassing wildlife after he kicked a barn owl while paragliding. Schanze, who originally denied the charges, faces one year of probation and had to forfeit his motorized flying device.

IDAHO: *My, my, what's in a name?* Arrested for allegedly stealing goods from unlocked cars in Boise was a young lady with quite a name: Amanda Miranda Panda. Panda and her boyfriend Tristen Parsons, both 18, were charged with three felony counts of burglary from automobiles. Authorities theorize that her name is derived from a once popular children's book, *Miranda the Panda is on the Veranda.*

IDAHO: *It's about time their Legislature did some meaningful work...* The Idaho Legislature has taken steps to get rid of a 151-year-old law giving Idaho authority if a person wounded in a duel in another stated dies within its borders. The original law was passed in 1864, after former vice President Aaron Burr and former treasury Secretary Alexander Hamilton sparred in a legendary New Jersey duel. Hamilton died in New York and both states charged Burr with murder.

COLORADO: *Bang, bang, nitwits.* Colorado Springs homeowner Christian Clark, 28, and his buddy Codie Leslie, 23, were drinking and taking target practice in Clark's makeshift basement shooting gallery. Police were called to the scene after neighbors heard gunfire coming from inside the house. No arrests were made but the police issued citations to the trigger happy young men.

ARIZONA: *Who Knew?* A chuckleheaded football fan was fired from his dream job working at Super Bowl XLIX, after he posted a photo of himself flashing his credentials on Facebook. Russ Knight, who was hired to work on a radio broadcast, got a call from NFL security a few hours after he posted the photo of himself. Officials explained that they were firing him because it was against the rules to post photos of Super Bowl credentials online due to duplication concerns.

NEW MEXICO: *There was certainly a "ceiling" to her intelligence...* A woman arrested and taken to a hospital for swallowing drugs, tried to escape custody by climbing through the hospital ceiling. She was missing for an hour before police found her up there.

OKLAHOMA: *But it could be such useful advice!* A history teacher was suspended late last year for posting a quote about cats in his classroom. Steven Alcorn could possibly lose his job for displaying a sign with the phrase, "In the dark, all cats are gray," a quote from Benjamin Franklin that encourages young men to sleep with older women. The quote, we learn, is taken from a letter dubbed: "Advice to a Young Man Choosing a Mistress," which authorities contend was much too racy for school. *MEEEOOOWW...*

THE END

About the Author

Professor Birdsong received his J.D. from the Harvard Law School and his B.A. from Howard University. He teaches law in Orlando, Florida.

After graduation from law school he worked four years at the law firm of Baker Hostetler. He then entered into a varied and distinguished career in government service. He served as a diplomat with the U.S. State Department with various postings in Nigeria, Germany and the Bahamas.

Professor Birdsong later served as a federal prosecutor. After leaving government service, and before he began teaching, Professor Birdsong was in private law practice in Washington, D.C.

www.BirdsongsLaw.com

lbirdsong@barry.edu

Ordering Information

New books coming soon!

Dear Reader,

If you liked this book, I would greatly appreciate you writing me a review on Amazon or any other book site.

I look forward to sharing more funny stories with you in future books.

Thank you, I really appreciate your help.

Regards,

Professor Birdsong

Winghurst Publications
1969 S. Alafaya Trail / Suite 303
Orlando, FL 32828-8732
www.BirdsongsLaw.com
lbirdsong@barry.edu

Other Books by Professor Birdsong:

* Professor Birdsong's 147 Dumbest Criminal Stories: Florida

* 177 Dumbest Criminal Stories – International

* Professor Birdsong's 157 Dumbest Criminal Stories (Kindle)

* Professor Birdsong's Weird Criminal Law Stories (Kindle)

* Professor Birdsong's "365" Weird Criminal Law Stories for Every Day of the Year (Kindle)

* Professor Birdsong's Weird Criminal Law Stories, Volume 2: Stories From Around the States and Abroad (Kindle)

* Professor Birdsong's Weird Criminal Law Stories, Volume 3: Stories from New York City and the East Coast. (Kindle)

* Professor Birdsong's Weird Criminal Law Stories - Volume 4: Stories from the Midwest (Kindle)

* Professor Birdsong's Weird Criminal Law Stories, Volume 5: Stories from Way Out West (Kindle)

* Professor Birdsong's Weird Criminal Law Stories - Volume 6: Women in Trouble (Kindle)

* Professor Birdsong's Weird Criminal Law - Volume 6: Women in Trouble! (Paperback)

* Immigration: Obama must act now! (Kindle)

Leonard Birdsong